Kyrie Irving

The amazing story of Kyrie Irving – one of basketball's most incredible players!

Table of Contents

Introduction

It is a warm evening in Newark, New Jersey. The Prudential Center in the heart of the city's business district is packed with young men and their families. There is a paradoxical air of excitement and nervousness. It is June 23, 2011 and the center is hosting the National Basketball Association's annual draft. The young men range from being teenagers to being in their early twenties. They are either a year out of high school or are university students. They are mostly from the United States, though there are a handful of players from outside of the country.

One of the players is a nineteen-year-old, who has recently completed one year as a student at Duke University. He is from the United States, though he was born in Australia. Even the most skilled journalist would have to prod him to jog his memory and ask him what emotions he felt. One can only wonder what thoughts were running through his mind. His future as a professional basketball player would be decided on that warm evening. If only he knew what was in store for him.

Who would have guessed that a young child living in the suburb of Kew in Melbourne, Australia would become one of the National Basketball Association's biggest stars? Perhaps Kyrie Irving himself may not have known, but he sure dreamed of it happening!

Today, Kyrie Andrew Irving is a twenty-something year old basketball player who has become a subject of admiration for any fan of the sport. He has soared with the Cleveland Cavaliers, continues to dominate with the Boston Celtics, and fans and experts alike are anticipating further accolades and milestones in his career.

Though he was born in Australia, Irving represented the United States in the 2014 FIBA Basketball World Cup. His dedication to the sport brought the team to victory, securing a Gold Medal. To top it off, he was named the MVP of the tournament. Not bad for a twenty-two-year-old!

He repeated this feat at the 2016 Summer Olympics, as Team USA secured a Gold Medal once again!

Lauded as one of the NBA's top Basketball players, he follows in the 'prodigy' tradition of a LeBron James.

Fast-forward to 2018 and Irving is now an All-Star Point Guard for the Boston Celtics, the team of the very city which his father Drederick has a connection to.

Yet, these attainments are just a small fraction of what makes Kyrie Irving the subject of adulation he is today. Apart from his presence on the court, he has also found fame in a series of Pepsi commercials, playing the character of Uncle Drew. In fact, Uncle Drew has found so much success, that Kyrie will be making his feature film debut as the character!

He has also gained notoriety by stating his conviction toward a few conspiracy theories, particularly noting that he believes the Earth is flat.

Kyrie Irving is not simply another great basketball player. He is an all-round entertainer, who serves to make his mark on the American cultural zeitgeist.

In just shy of three decades, his life tells a fascinating story.

Of course, this fascinating story, like all stories of such magnitude, has a surprisingly humble beginning.

Chapter 1: Beginning Down Under, Rising To The Top

In this chapter you will learn about Kyrie Irving's childhood, his father's influence over him, and the early years of playing basketball – before he made it to the big leagues.

Kew is a suburb in Melbourne, Australia. It boasts a population of 23,000. However, this small suburb is not without its fascinating stories. It has its fair share of business persons, politicians, and athletes. One such story, involves an American athlete who is in the spotlight today.

Kyrie Andrew Irving's love for basketball, is owed to his father Drederick Irving. The senior Irving was himself a basketball player for Boston University, and upon matriculation moved to Australia to play for the Bulleen Boomers. Naturally, his love for the sport was passed on to his children – with the young Kyrie showing promise.

Promise.

This is an important word for Kyrie Irving. As a child, he made a secret pact with his sister Asia, that he would play for the NBA. He wrote as a fourth-grader:

I'm going to the NBA

Promise

Despite the optimism, early life for the Irving family was not the easiest. Elizabeth Irving, Drederick's wife, and mother to his children passed away at the young age of 29, with Sepsis Syndrome and a multisystem organ failure contributing to her untimely death.

With the hardship of being a single father, the senior Irving found comfort in basketball. Though he eventually stopped playing professionally, his love for the sport never faded, and it was passed to his children. His son, Kyrie, seemed to particularly take a shining to basketball.

Though born in Kew, Kyrie returned to the United States with his family at the age of two. It was when he was four that his mother passed, leaving Drederick to raise his children on his own. Their relationship remains a close one. Kyrie states, "He is my father first. But he's also like my big brother and my best friend."

Now permanently settled in the United States, Kyrie does not recall his first two years in Australia but maintains a close relationship with the nation. He travels there occasionally and has coached basketball for young children in Melbourne.

Yet basketball was not young Kyrie's first love. Oddly enough, there was another sport which first caught his eye.

Getting On Board

Originally trying out rollerblading, Kyrie eventually graduated to skateboarding. This became his first sport of choice. Skateboarding culture must have been popular in West Orange, New Jersey because Kyrie was not alone. He recalls obsessing over buying his first skateboard, with trucks and wheels, and attempting to build mini-ramps in his backyard. His friend and neighbor Daniel had a small plastic ramp, on which him and Kyrie would practice their tricks – always trying to land the perfect Ollie.

For reasons he cannot entirely recall, Kyrie's cousin and Daniel once got into a fight as the three guys were skating. As a result, this terminated the skating sessions at Daniel's house; However, this did not stop the young Kyrie from trying to land the perfect Ollie. He attempted one upon returning home, and not only did he fail – but it was to be his final attempt!

Kyrie attempted to Ollie over a rock, and to his chagrin, failed and landed knee-first on another rock! The injury was serious and required stitches. However, his knee was not the only thing that got damaged. Frustrated with Kyrie, Drederick grabbed the skateboard and broke it! The relationship between Kyrie Irving and his beloved skateboard, had tragically ended.

As painful as a knee injury and a broken skateboard may be to a young child, this was perhaps a blessing in disguise, as it meant that basketball was once again part of Kyrie's life.

Back On Court

There was not a particular time when basketball was introduced to Kyrie Irving. Because of Drederick's history and love for the sport, basketball was always there. As a result, the affection toward the sport would often dwindle.

A dark time was when Drederick felt young Kyrie, though adept at the sport, was not taking it as seriously as one should. In his anger, Kyrie gathered his basketball trophies in a box and smashed them. His father, though disappointed, did not stop his son from discarding the trophies. Kyrie left the box with the smashed trophies outside. Though the garbage truck came by the house, they refused to collect the box with the trophies. After calming down, Kyrie fetched the box and returned it to the house – where it remains to this day!

Despite the ups and downs, basketball was to continue.

The dedication to the sport moved beyond one-on-one between father and son. Soon enough, Kyrie had other opponents. Thanks to his father's legacy at Boston University, Kyrie began his serious training at the school's summer basketball camps. He later graduated to playing with the Amateur Athletic Union. It was here that he was noticed by high school basketball coach Tony Jones.

Jones recognized the teenager's adeptness for the sport. Jones spotted a potential mentee in Kyrie Irving, and his vision came true. The young teenager attended Montclair Kimberley Academy, and naturally flourished in basketball under Jones' wing.

The freshman was a key to the basketball team of Montclair Kimberley Academy; however, there was potential for more growth. In his sophomore year, he transferred to St. Patrick High School.

It is fair to say, this was when the living legend began his road to stardom.

The Hero of St. Patrick

While Montclair helped Kyrie hone his skills on the court, it was his time at St. Patrick which caught everyone's eye. Chris Chavannes, the basketball team's coach, confidently praised Kyrie Irving as being an All-Star player for the team.

The transition to the new school, however, was not the easiest. Montclair Kimberley Academy was a prestigious preparatory school. It remains a beacon of education, preparing its students for Higher Education and future success. It was at this institution where Kyrie Irving began his training; however, it was at St. Patrick High School where he began his road to stardom.

A hero of the NBA, as a Celtic and as a Cavalier prior to that, started out as The Hero of St. Patrick.

St. Patrick remains recognized for its stellar basketball program. However, at the time the school was known to be a school that attracted delinquents. Furthermore, Kyrie describes the area of Elizabeth, New Jersey as 'the hood'. Each afternoon, after being dismissed from school, Kyrie would take a two-and-a-half-hour bus ride to return home. While this may seem exhausting for any teenager, there was a reason for the commitment to the bus ride, and to the commitment to transferring to the less-prestigious school. It was the basketball program.

Upon transferring to St. Patrick High School, Kyrie was placed among the top 100 high-school basketball players in the United States. His rank gradually increased from 82 to being amongst the top 3 players. It was his performance on the court which led to this prestigious stamp on his resume.

From a Fighting Celtic, he was to become a Blue Devil...

Chapter Summary

• This American basketball player was actually born in Australia! His love for the sport rises from his father's background.

• After one-on-one practice with the senior Irving, Kyrie began his training at Boston University's summer camps.

• He joined St. Patrick High School, which is where his road to stardom began.

In the next chapter you will learn how playing basketball for St. Patrick High School would lead to playing college basketball – the sign of bigger things to come!

Chapter 2: The Cavalier Kyrie Irving

In this chapter you will learn how Kyrie Irving graduated from St. Patrick High School to enroll in Duke University. Duke, however, would be short-lived as bigger things were to come!

Kyrie Irving led the Fighting Celtics of St. Patrick High School to victory in the New Jersey Tournament of Champions. This prominent tournament recognizes the best teams in their appropriate sports, and it was under young Kyrie's wing that the Fighting Celtics won their third title. He later played for Team USA East in the Nike Global Challenge – again, leading the team to the tournament title.

Unfortunately, in his senior year of high school, Kyrie was unable to lead the Fighting Celtics to another victory in the New Jersey Tournament of Champions. Violating The New Jersey State Interscholastic Athletic Association's, coach Kevin Boyle attended the basketball teams' workout sessions. As a result, the team was disqualified from participating in the tournament.

While this may have been a disappointment for Kyrie Irving and the Fighting Celtics, more opportunities were to come his way – perhaps opportunities he dreamed of, but never imagined he would have! He committed to attending Duke University, and it was there where his journey as a professional basketball player would take off.

He graduated as a Fighting Celtic and was promoted to a Blue Devil. At Duke University he, almost predictably, excelled at the game; His achievements were not only stellar for a college athlete, but particularly for a freshman. During his freshman year in 2010-2011, he was only the fourth freshman to score over thirty points in a single game! Needless to say, one-on-one with Drederick, Boston University summer camps, Montclair and St. Patrick's prepared Kyrie Irving for his almost-celebrity status at Duke University.

Kyrie has fond memories of his time at Duke but recalls the intensity of training. Kyrie was almost a phenomenon; he was a top high-school level basketball player. However, his coach at Duke did not allow the young Kyrie to rest on his laurels. Kyrie recalls his coach putting him on a 'Muscle Milk Diet' and forbidding him from frequenting Shooters – a local bar which was patronized by many Duke undergraduates.

Coach Mike Krzyzewski, affectionately dubbed 'Coach Handy', helped Kyrie improve particular skills of his. Despite his success at the sport, there were still various aspects of his athleticism that needed to be worked on. One of these was his handling.

Handling, of course, is the skill of how one dribbles a basketball. Even as a young child, Drederick would lecture Kyrie on the need to improve his handling skills, among many others. "You are not taking this seriously!", he would quip to his son. Coach Handy helped Kyrie master dribbling the ball, pivoting, and crossing-over. On a podcast interview with fellow player J.J. Redick, Kyrie was praised by Redick on his superb handling skills. Kyrie Irving has been fortunate to have a slew of great coaches, but it was Coach Handy who helped him master his handles!

While winning or perhaps playing for fun may have been Kyrie Irving's attitude toward basketball, it was his time with Coach Handy which made him understand the art of the sport; he would later refer to this as the poetry of the sport. In the same discussion with Redick, the two masters of their craft realized that the difference between playing for fun and playing professionally, was the entertainment and artistic value that a player owed to their audience. He may or may not have realized it then, but Kyrie was a natural entertainer and had been bitten by the creative bug.

Kyrie's accomplishments at Duke University are remembered to this day; any basketball fan would not hesitate to rattle-off statistics: he only played eleven games, as he missed out on twenty-six due to a toe injury; managed two steals; thirty-one points against Michigan State; and the list goes on. All of this, in one year of university. The future was bright, and as one looks back, they will notice that Kyrie Irving did not complete his studies at Duke University. His time as a Blue Devil was short-lived. But this was not a tragedy; this was the beginning of his career with the National Basketball Association.

Goodbye Durham, Hello Cleveland!

Missing out on twenty-six games due to a toe injury! Needless to say, this would have been a dark time in any basketball player's professional life. Yet Kyrie Irving remembers this time fondly: he even goes as far as to say that that time in his career made him fall in love with Duke University. While he was off the court, his teammates remained close by.

He would spend time with them, exploring the campus of Duke University, and the town of Durham – perhaps even frequenting Shooters! They also attended plays, and Kyrie took a few acting classes – something which would come in handy in later years. When his teammates had to call it a night to practice basketball early the next morning, Kyrie began wandering on his own: on his crutches, of course! The exploration of life made Kyrie a versatile individual, these talents would be exposed to the public later, after he became a basketball star. And becoming a star was just around the corner.

Kyrie Irving was now nineteen-years-old. He had been out of high school for a year and had completed a year at Duke University. This made him eligible for the National Basketball Association's Draft. While he was excited, as any aspiring player would be, he was slightly reluctant to participate in the draft. As with all university freshman, he wanted to experience the college lifestyle, at least for one more year. Additionally, there was another concern - he had only played eleven games at Duke University. He felt he was unprepared to play in the big leagues.

The senior Irving had more confidence.

He assured his son that it was time for the draft. There was nothing more to learn in one more year of being a Blue Devil. It was time to play for a city.

With his father, sister Asia, friends Kevin and Elijah as his entourage, Kyrie Irving went to the Prudential Center in Newark, New Jersey to attend the 2011 NBA Draft on the Twenty-Third of June. Sixty players were drafted, from the United States and from abroad. They were drafted for various teams across the country. The Cleveland Cavaliers had first pick and chose four players.

In his famous book How To Win Friends and Influence People, Dale Carnegie had written, "Names are the sweetest and most important sound in any language."

When the first pick of the draft was called, Carnegie's statement had perhaps never rung truer for Kyrie.

Kyle Irving was the first pick, and at the tender age of nineteen, after only spending a year as a Blue Devil at Duke University, he had now become the Point Guard for the Cleveland Cavaliers.

Quite a long way from Kew, isn't it?

Chapter Summary

• From St. Patrick High School, Kyrie graduated to attend Duke University.

• It was during his time at the University that he improved his craft and learned about the art of the sport. He also developed interests outside of the field which will later impact other career decisions.

• To his surprise, he was the first pick of the NBA Draft and was welcomed as a nineteen-year-old to play for the Cleveland Cavaliers.

In the next chapter you will learn how Kyrie realized there were greater expectations in the NBA than he could have imagined.

However, this did not worry him, and he was determined to lead his new team to the NBA Championship.

Chapter 3: Road To The Championship

In this chapter you will learn how, despite hurdles and the immense pressure thrust upon him, Kyrie Irving was determined to make his mark with the Cavaliers and lead them to victory.

The city of Cleveland is an exciting metropolis in the heart of Ohio. It has a rich history of athleticism: from Olympic runner Jesse Owens, who grew up in the city, to the Cleveland Indians in baseball, the Cleveland Browns in football, and of course the Cleveland Cavaliers in basketball.

In recent years, the Cavaliers have received several accolades in the NBA. The team won Conference titles in 2007, 2015, 2016 and 2017.

One of the team's recent stars is LeBron James. LeBron was seen as a 'prodigy', a young man excelling at the sport amongst older men. However, in 2011, another young prodigy was to join the team, and was taken under LeBron's wing.

No Boys Allowed

In one interview, a few years into his professional career, Kyrie Irving quipped that the NBA stood for, "No Boys Allowed." Perhaps this was due to the fact that he understood the graduation from being a high-school or college-level athlete, to a professional athlete. Being one of the youngest recruits to the team, he soon had to learn how to shape up.

He recalls how playing basketball for forty minutes with his friends could tire him. Such a feeling was prohibited in the professional league. Fondly recalling how he was pushed around, how he had to get into shape – as he still possessed the physique of a college student, as opposed to a professional player.

He felt that at the beginning of his start with the Cavaliers, himself and the other rookies existed solely for the senior players to practice with. But these reminisces are not filled with regret – Kyrie sees these as learning opportunities, and necessary to his growth as a basketball player.

However, it didn't take long for Kyrie to create his legacy with the Cleveland Cavaliers.

Just as he stood out as an outstanding freshman in high school, and repeated the feat at Duke University, within his first year with the Cavaliers, he won the NBA Rookie of the Year award for 2012. Furthermore, he was selected for the NBA All-Rookie First Team. The Cavalier Point Guard was getting the notice he was accustomed to, however, this time it was on a much larger scale!

While he damaged his hand during a practice session with the team, and later injured a finger during a match against the Dallas Mavericks, this did not stop him from achieving great heights in the game. His highest achievement was in a match against the New York Knicks where he scored 41 points, his highest to date. While the match to the Knicks ended in a loss for the Cavaliers, Kyrie became the youngest player to score over 40 points in Madison Square Garden. The record he beat, was that of Michael Jordan's!

Naturally, his accolades did not go unnoticed. Once again, his coaches showed him support and granted him future opportunities. He was selected to play for his first All-Star game in 2013. He also played (though sadly lost) for Team Shaq in the Rising Stars Challenge; and won the NBA Three-Point Shootout, by scoring 23 points in the final round.

One of the Cavs

With his achievements with the Cavaliers, it was clear that this Australian-born, Jersey-bred athlete was now a son of Cleveland! LeBron James returned from the Miami Heat to rejoin the Cavaliers; and Kyrie Irving signed an extended contract to continue to play for the team. The contract was for $90-million, solidifying the 22-year-old as a hot commodity in the world of basketball. As Kevin Love requested to be traded to the Cavaliers from the Minnesota Timberwolves, the team now had three of the NBA's most-adept players. The three players became known as, 'The Big Three'.

Even as The Big Three showed promise, the Cavaliers were off to a rocky beginning. While they narrowly defeated the Charlotte Hornets 91-87, with both Kyrie Irving and Kevin Love scoring over twenty points, the team's winning-streak was short-lived. They were soon defeated by the Dallas Mavericks. Later, Irving missed the match against the Philadelphia 76'ers, and though he returned for a match against the Houston Rockets, the Cavaliers lost, adding another defeat to their record.

2015 showed more promise. Kyrie Irving stepped his game up, as did LeBron James and the Cavaliers went from a losing-streak to 12-game winning streak! They made it to the NBA finals, but lost the championship to the Golden State Warriors. Despite the loss, the Cavaliers felt a sense of pride, and optimism was high for the team amongst its players and amongst fans. The Big Three were noticed, but Kyrie Irving in particular was noticed – his tremendous skill at a young age reminded fans of LeBron James himself.

We Are The Champions

As a young skater, Kyrie Irving failed an attempt to Ollie, and split his kneecap over a rock. He must have thought to himself, this is the last time this will happen!

Sadly, it was not! He had acquired (unwittingly, of course) a fractured kneecap during a game in the 2015 NBA finals. While he had to sit out many games, he returned to the court in December of 2015, and went on to establish his place in basketball history.

In his first match against the Philadelphia 76'ers, he made an impression by scoring 12 points in a short span of 17 minutes! In the first match of the new year, 2016, he scored 32 points against the Washington Wizards – which became a season high and helped the Cavaliers defeat the Wizards! Clearly, these 32 points were not enough for Kyrie as he beat his record by three points only two days later, this time helping the Cavaliers defeat the Los Angeles Lakers.

After many successful games, the Cavaliers were in the finals again. Ironically or perhaps fortuitously, they were once again playing against the Golden State Warriors. All eyes were on these two teams, with two major questions: Would the Golden State Warriors continue to reign, or would the Cleveland Cavaliers redeem themselves and become the NBA Champions?

Game 1: The first game was close for much of the game, but finished 104-89. Unfortunately, for the Cleveland Cavaliers, the 104 was granted to the Golden State Warriors. While the Cavaliers were ahead for the first half of the game, the Golden State Warriors broke through in the third and fourth quarters. There was a personal victory however for Kyrie Irving, as he led the scoring with 26 points. However, this was not enough, and the Cavaliers had to accept defeat.

Game 2: This game was perhaps a greater disappointment. While The Big Three were determined to redeem themselves, Kevin Love suffered a head injury during the game, and sat out for the second half of the game. Kyrie and LeBron were determined to continue without any further hindrance, and though LeBron led with 19 points, Kyrie did not make a significant contribution to this match. From high school to his professional career, Kyrie Irving was known to make his mark in a game, whether his team won or not, yet this game was a dark moment in his career. To make matters worse, despite the best efforts of the Cavaliers, this was their second loss to the Golden State Warriors. The final score was 110-77, a significantly greater gap than Game 1.

One can only imagine what the morale of the Cleveland Cavaliers was after these two harrowing losses. While LeBron James had found championship success before, Kyrie Irving was sure to have felt an overwhelming sense of disappointment. He had become accustomed to being a star, from his high-school days to his year at Duke University, to being the first pick at the 2011 NBA Draft.

In his second year with the Cleveland Cavaliers, it looked like the team would face another defeat. While he made contributions throughout, he was not leading them to victory. There must have been moments of self-doubt; he must have thought that the Golden State Warriors would once again claim victory.

But of course, Kyrie Irving did not and does not give up. One wonders if he recalled smashing his basketball trophies at a low point and frustration with the sport. Did he reflect on how he moved on from that incident and pondered how the child who smashed his trophies became the top pick in the NBA Draft, and went on to sign a $90 million contract?

Perhaps we shall never know. But what we do know, is that in spite of the upsetting two games, Kyrie Irving was determined to lead the Cleveland Cavaliers to victory. He certainly made that impression, with Game 3.

Game 3: Kevin Love had to sit out the game due to a concussion. However, this obstacle did not seem to faze the team, and certainly not it's star players Kyrie Irving and LeBron James. The first quarter left Cleveland's fans in an uproar! Leading by 17 points, it looked like the team was ready to retaliate for the two prior losses. LeBron James scored a game-high 32 points, and Kyrie Irving scored 30 points – making an important. Although Golden State caught up in the second quarter, the Cavaliers still lead the game, though only by a few points. But by the end of the game, the Cavaliers were still beating the Warriors. Victory belonged to the Cleveland Cavaliers, and skeptics and naysayers were reminded of the second question: Would the Cleveland Cavaliers redeem themselves and become the NBA Champions?

Game 4: Clearly, the Cleveland Cavaliers had struck a nerve with the Golden State Warriors. Though they were leading, they were in a state of tension. They could no longer rest on their laurels; it was possible that the Cavaliers would win this game, and that they would even the series at 2 games apiece. The high scorer for the game was the Warriors' Stephen Curry, who scored a total of 38 points. They also set a record for scoring more three-pointers (17) than two-pointers (16); a first in NBA Finals history. Kyrie Irving was the star of the Cavaliers that day. He scored 34 points, just a couple baskets shy of Stephen Curry's score.

While this showed that Kyrie and the Cavaliers were back in the game, the Warriors still managed to score a victory, narrowly defeating the Cavaliers, 108 points to 97. A notable point of this game was when the Warriors' Draymond Green fell to the floor. Whether intentionally or not, LeBron James stepped over him, and an infuriated Green hit the Cavalier in the groin. This caused them to be kept apart for the remainder of the game. Needless to say, tensions were high. Though this was a victory for the Warriors, the Cavaliers played a close game, and the Warriors were in no position to get comfortable. The Warriors now lead the Cavaliers in the series 3-1.

Game 5: Perhaps Kyrie Irving was determined to not only win this next game, but also mercilessly outdo Stephen Curry. Whether intentional or not, it worked exactly in that manner. Stephen Curry was the top scorer for the Warriors, scoring 25 points. In response, both Kyrie Irving and LeBron James scored 41 points each. Kyrie wasn't backing down and he ensured the Cavaliers had another victory – with a final score of 112 points to 97 points.

Game 6: It seems that a personal battle between Kyrie Irving and Stephen Curry was in order. Not only were the two Point Guards determined to lead their teams to victory, they also seemed to want to score more baskets than the other player. In this battle, Curry won – scoring 30 points to Irving's 23. Despite his scoring performance, Curry's reign was short-lived. He had accumulated several fouls over the course of the game, and in his anger threw his mouthpiece into the stands. He was removed for the remainder of the match. Perhaps this was a blessing in disguise, as the Cavaliers won the game 115 points to 101 points.

Game 7: The series was tied at 3 games apiece, with only one game remaining. The two teams were reunited again to battle for the NBA Championship. One team wished to repeat their victory from the previous year; another wished to avenge the title and become the champions for the first time. To top it off, this was the first time in the history of the NBA when two teams had a total of the same amount of points come game 7: 610. The competition could not be more even.

Fans of both teams were on the edge of their seats. The players from both sides were tense. The young Point Guard for the Cleveland Cavaliers was especially in a mixed state of glee and uncertainty.

He had been faced with challenges throughout his basketball career, but none of this magnitude. He had led the Montclair Kimberley Academy Cougars, the St. Patrick High School Fighting Celtics, and Duke University's Blue Devils. Along with LeBron James, would he be able to lead the Cleveland Cavaliers to victory?

After halftime, the Warriors were in the lead – though barely – with a score of 49 points to 42 points. Both teams were nervous, and though the Warriors were leading, this was not the time to be comfortable – as the Cavaliers were close behind. The supposed competition between Kyrie Irving and Stephen Curry had not come to an end: they still appeared to outdo each other with every play. While LeBron scored 27 points, Kyrie Irving was a point behind and managed to beat Stephen Curry's overall points: 17.

The Cavaliers were ahead after the third quarter, however, with less than five minutes left in the final quarter, both teams were tied at 89 points. Time was ticking, yet LeBron managed to score a three pointer and later made a free throw.

LeBron James was named the MVP of the series as he brought the Cleveland Cavaliers to victory. However, on reflection, one cannot discount the contribution of the young Kyrie Irving, who, as part of The Big Three, helped lead the team to victory. It was safe to say that though much of the spotlight was on LeBron James, the player from West Orange, New Jersey had also become a hero for the city of Cleveland. Together, they were the first team to come back from a 3-1 series deficit to win an NBA championship!

Kyrie Irving had become a hero of the National Basketball Association. There was no turning back now. LeBron James, once seen as the young wonder kid of basketball had perhaps unknowingly passed this title on to Kyrie Irving. And sure enough, Drederick Irving was proud that his son reached heights he never did.

Chapter Summary

• Despite initial struggles, Kyrie did not give up and he would not rest until he led the Cavaliers to victory.

• Thanks to Kyrie's assistance the Cleveland Cavaliers won their first NBA Championship.

• Kyrie Irving signed an extended $90-million dollar contract to continue to play with his new team.

In the next chapter you will learn how Kyrie felt that there were better opportunities elsewhere, and how leaving the Cavaliers caused tension between him and LeBron James.

Chapter 4: Back To Boston

In this chapter you will learn about the media frenzy when Kyrie announced he would leave the Cavaliers for the Celtics, and his reasons for doing so.

Stephen A. Smith to Kyrie, "Do you believe you can win without LeBron James?"

Kyrie replies, "Time will tell."

Stephen A. Smith retorts, "I asked you what you believe."

Kyrie Irving responds simply with, "Oh, absolutely."

The Cleveland Cavaliers and the entire city had much to celebrate on June 19, 2017. They had become the NBA Champions, and an energy of joy and exuberance was rampant around the city. Though all players were responsible for leading the team to victory, the highest recognition was given to LeBron James. He was chosen as the MVP and became the hero of Cleveland. Kyrie Irving's contribution did not go unnoticed, yet in the aftermath of the game, it seemed to be overshadowed by LeBron's success. Kyrie decided it was time for a change.

The city of Boston has always had a place in Kyrie Irving's heart. Boston University was Drederick Irving's alma matter. The senior Irving is remembered fondly as a hero of the Boston University Terriers. It is also at Boston University where Kyrie had his initial basketball training, apart from one-on-one sessions with his father. Since the city has always been close to him, it was almost predictable that he would wish to eventually play for the Boston Celtics.

In his first press conference as a player for the Boston Celtics, Kyrie fondly recalls growing up watching the Boston Celtics play. He reminds a wave of inquisitive journalists that he was nineteen-years-old and had barely completed a year of university when he was drafted into the NBA. However, the six years traveling to different cities with the Cleveland Cavaliers made him grow up quickly and made him realize that off-court he should aim for something larger than himself. Ultimately, it was about being the best basketball player he could be.

The switch to the Boston Celtics came as a surprise to many, and the surprise was not pleasant. The media began to speculate as to why Kyrie Irving decided to trade himself to another team. Within days, the question arose as to whether Kyrie wished to step away from LeBron James.

The Cleveland Cavaliers had been good to Kyrie Irving, and now that he had joined another team, he had to figure out how to defeat a team which he himself helped reach victory.

Appearing on First Take to discuss his thoughts on the trade, Kyrie was presented with several hard-hitting questions. On the show, he was grilled by Stephen A. Smith as to why he chose to leave a team which had been so good to him. Kyrie kept his composure and professionally shared his viewpoint. His desire was to grow as a basketball player and to perfect his craft, and he felt that an opportunity to play with the Boston Celtics would provide him with a platform for such growth. When asked if he consulted or informed LeBron James on his decision, he stated that he did not and furthermore, he did not feel the need to do so.

While this logic seemed sufficient for Kyrie Irving, the media still was not convinced. After the initial grilling by Stephen A. Smith, Max Kellerman joined the discussion on First Take and pressed Kyrie on why he left the Cavaliers without informing LeBron. Kyrie responded with a question as to why so much attention was given to one player, when it was an entire team that Kyrie was leaving behind.

Kellerman proceeded to ask if there was a personal issue with LeBron or any other member of the Cavaliers that had not become public knowledge. He did not state in the affirmative. He made it clear there was nothing personal. Remaining calm and collected, Kyrie stated that he did not feel he owed anyone anything and this was a personal decision, and in his mind, the best decision for his career.

On ESPN, a debate sparked as to whether or not Kyrie Irving was at fault for not informing LeBron James prior to his decision to leave the Cavaliers. The frenzy seemed as if it would rage on, but gradually it came to a close. At a press conference, LeBron was asked about his thoughts on the trade. He stated that he experienced a whirlwind of emotions, but ultimately respected Kyrie's decision and wished him well.

Back On The Court

Once it was time for Kyrie Irving to get back on the court, the attention moved away from the trade, and all eyes were eager to see how Kyrie would perform with the Boston Celtics. And what a debut it was! The first match that Irving played in was against the Cleveland Cavaliers! Kyrie scored 22 points and the game was a close one – the Cavaliers led by three points, totaling 102 points over the Celtics 99. As fate would have it, it was left to Kyrie to score a three-pointer at the end of the game to tie the scores and take the teams into overtime.

He missed, and his first game as a Celtic against his former team resulted in a loss.

But of course, this loss did not stop the formidable Point Guard. Almost two weeks after the match against the Cleveland Cavaliers, Kyrie helped the Celtics defeat the San Antonio Spurs. In early November, he helped them defeat the Atlanta Hawks, and once again, two weeks later he led the team in defeating the Dallas Mavericks.

Before the closing of November, the Celtics were defeated by the Miami Heat. In the beginning of 2018, they suffered two more losses: one to the Orlando Magic, and the second to the Golden State Warriors. As a Cavalier, Kyrie helped the team redeem themselves and defeat the Warriors in the NBA Championship, yet in his first season as a Celtic, he was defeated by the

Cavaliers as well as the Warriors. However, during the season the Celtics also had a solid winning-streak, and speculation as to whether Kyrie's future with the Boston Celtics would be bright was in full effect.

As he stated on First Take after being interrogated by Stephen A. Smith: "Time will tell."

Chapter Summary

• Controversy arose as many felt that Kyrie's departure from the Cavaliers was sudden, and that it may have been due to a personal issue with LeBron James.

• Kyrie was determined to perfect his craft and lead the Celtics to the Championship.

• While the Celtics lost to both the Cavaliers and the Warriors, Kyrie did bring them some success. It is perhaps too early for one to know what the future holds.

In the next chapter you will learn about who Kyrie Irving is off the court. He is not simply just another basketball player: he is a versatile individual, and he is about to show the world what else he is capable of!

Chapter 5: Off Season, Off Court

In this chapter you will learn how Kyrie used his artistic talents to create a fictitious character that the world would come to love. We'll also discuss a statement he made which has caused quite a stir.

Basketball players come and go. The ones who leave a legacy become an extension of their athleticism. Their personalities off court and off season, become as prominent as their skills on court during the season. Michael Jordan, Shaquille O'Neal, Kobe Bryant, and LeBron James are a few names that belong to this short list. Kyrie Andrew Irving is the latest name to be added.

Being born in a foreign country, living in different cities in the United States, attending two different high schools, and spending a year at the prestigious Duke University seems to have left an impression on Kyrie. It has contributed to his sense of curiosity; it is this curiosity which he displays in his interviews and public appearances. His thoughts and viewpoints have been inspirational for some of the public, and have also come under mass scrutiny by others.

He recalls his time at Duke University when he missed playing several games due to an injury. While this kept him off the court for some time, it allowed him to explore other aspects of his curious mind, and flourish in them.

He possesses an insatiable thirst for knowledge and particularly for artistic expression. In an interview with actor and businessman Chris 'Drama' Pfaff, he cheerfully remembers seeing plays with his teammates and even taking a few acting classes. Just as his basketball practice with his father led to a professional career, it seems that those few acting classes made a similar impact.

Youngbloods, Meet Uncle Drew

On a dark night, a van drives through the empty streets of Bloomfield, New Jersey. Seated in the back of the van is an elderly gentleman with snow-white hair, glasses, and a slight hunchback. Dressed in a sweatshirt and sweatpants, he is rambling about basketball. He states how he 'came up in the real time' and boasts about his adeptness at the sport. As he pulls up to Clark's Pond Courts he states that the younger generation is obsessed with their 'rappity-hippity hop' and their sneakers. He is determined to show them the fundamentals of the game.

After a few sneers by an audience on the basketball court, the gentleman scores 'bucket after bucket' and shows the 'youngbloods' how it's done. The elderly gentleman is named Uncle Drew, and a non-discerning view may ponder how a man of his age can still play the game so well. But if one looks with a sharp eye, they notice that this is the first of a series of short films produced by Pepsi, starring the Boston Celtics Point Guard - Kyrie Irving!

In what was his first endorsement – Kyrie's stint with acting classes paid off. The four Uncle Drew short films have garnered the attention and love from the public; in the tradition of Michael Jordan in Space Jam and Shaquille O'Neal in Kazaam, Kyrie Irving has brought the eponymous character to a feature film being released in 2018.

Kyrie Irving has not been a stranger to controversy. His first brush was with the immense scrutiny on his sudden departure to the Cavaliers, and whether there were personal issues with LeBron James or a hidden desire to step out of the former teammate's shadow. However, no media expert could have predicted this next unusual controversy.

On an appearance with former Cleveland Cavaliers teammates Richard Jefferson and Channing Frye on their podcast Road Trippin' with RJ and Channing, the trio were discussing "This is not even a conspiracy theory... The Earth is flat. The Earth is flat... It's right in front of our faces. I'm telling you, it's right in front of our faces. They lie to us."

Kyrie Irving

conspiracy theories, when the conspiracy that the Earth is flat came up. To everyone's shock, Kyrie remarked:

Initially seeming to be a joke, controversy arose when the media and the public realized that Kyrie was serious about his convictions. His statement has been ridiculed, and concerns that he believes the Earth is flat have been soaring. Many wished to dismiss it as a joke, yet Kyrie Irving remains stringent about his belief. When pressed on the issue he repeats that he feels there is much that is not being taught, that he believes he understands science and there is evidence to his claims.

On an appearance on Jimmy Kimmel Live, host Jimmy Kimmel asked him about his conviction. Once again, Kyrie stated that he has an understanding about the Earth and that the public should not believe blindly in what they are taught. Jimmy Kimmel humorously presented him with a round basketball in the design of a globe. Kyrie smiled and took the ball, yet one wonders if his belief remains strong.

Staying Humble

In spite of the recent controversies, Kyrie Irving is genuinely liked by the basketball fraternity and by the general public. Even though Jimmy Kimmel may have playfully mocked him about his Flat Earth beliefs, he thoroughly seemed to enjoy his conversation with the affable basketball player.

In the celebrity culture that pervades the United States, it is not uncommon to see erratic behavior from an athlete who has reached a level of success. If the athlete is young and has a large bank balance, we may see them flaunt their extravagance and their stature. Yet we do not see this in Kyrie Irving. While he enjoys life and goes out to celebrate his success, it has not brought a sense of arrogance to him. He recalls partying hard after being selected as the top pick for the NBA Draft, yet was not resistant to the pushing around and intense training that the

NBA required of him. Despite the success he had attained as an amateur athlete, he knew there was room to grow, and this has helped him succeed in the professional league.

His friends have also had a great influence on him. He recalls how one friend gave him the book Emotions by Osho, which he claims helped him become less stubborn. His interest in philosophy continued with the writings of J. Krishnamurti. He states that these books made him realize there was no need to be afraid to ask for help, and by asking for help he would gain knowledge that other individuals have gained.

Now with a daughter of his own, he realizes that his priorities have changed – just as Drederick realized when his own children were born. While his career is important to him, he is aware of the world-at-large and that he experiences a life outside of the realm of professional Basketball.

Chapter Summary

• Owing to the time in University where he explored other facets of life, he was able to express his creativity to the world.

• Through a series of short films produced by Pepsi and an upcoming feature, he has introduced us to the lovable character Uncle Drew.

• He has caused an unusual controversy by stating he believes the Earth is flat.

In the next chapter you will learn in greater detail how Drederick Irving helped shape Kyrie Irving to the athlete and individual he is today.

Chapter 6: Like Father, Like Son

In this chapter you will learn who Drederick Irving is, what his upbringing was like, and why Kyrie Irving considers him to be not only a father, but a best friend.

It is the summer of 2017, and the twenty-five-year-old Kyrie Irving is having a relaxed chat on Chris Pfaff's podcast. He recollects his childhood, his high school basketball career, and the wild celebration once he was drafted into the NBA. Later on, the tone changes.

Pfaff humbly asks one of the sport's superstars if he ever has doubts. He asks if there is ever a moment when the stellar Point Guard Kyrie Irving is on the court and wants to give it all up.

Kyrie takes a deep breath and lets out a loud sigh. "It's gotten to that point. I think every human being goes through that point…" He looks back on those dark days where he did not feel like getting out of bed to practice. Athletes are often presented in a powerful manner. Male athletes are even shown in an almost hyper-masculine fashion; their vulnerabilities are hidden from the public eye. Yet this simple question from Chris Pfaff seemed to have struck a chord with Kyrie Irving.

Professional basketball players are in a position of privilege. They live a lifestyle that is envied by others. How many 22-year-olds are signing a $90-million contract? Not only was Kyrie Irving drafted into the National Basketball Association after his first year at Duke University, he was also the first pick of the evening. Still in his twenties he has partnered with Pepsi for the Uncle Drew short films, and the feature film is to come. Yet, there remains a humility in the young Kyrie Irving. It is because he sees a world outside of the sport, and it is a world with its own troubles that he very much has to live in. His position of privilege does not seem to exempt him from the worries of life.

Pfaff proceeds to ask him, "Did you have a mentor of any kind?"

There is a slight pause, until Kyrie realizes that the answer is an obvious one. "My dad has consistently been in that mentor role…"

The senior Irving had found fame with basketball: first with the Boston University Terriers. He was, at one point, the top scorer for the team and had been named Most Valuable Player. His attainments with the team provided him a permanent place in the Boston University Athletic Hall of Fame. If one were to list the statistics of Drederick's achievements at Boston University, it may cause him embarrassment: he scored an average of twenty points per game; he was the top scorer for three years in a row; he brought the Terriers to participate in the 1987 ECAC North Atlantic tournament, losing by a mere three points to Northeastern University. Probably his only disappointment was being defeated in the NCAA Tournament – ironically by what would become his son's alma matter, Duke University!

Little did Drederick know that his next opportunity in basketball would be through a Boston University Alumnus. Brett Brown was coaching a team called the Bulleen Boomers in the city of Melbourne, Australia. He found success with the team, though ultimately, they lost to Sydney in the SEABL Finals.

Drederick Irving never lost his passion for the game, though it was not pursued professionally after leaving the Bulleen Boomers. He was settled in Australia and began his family there. With his wife Elizabeth, they welcomed daughter Asia as the first addition to the Irving family. Then on March 23, 1992 they welcomed their son, Kyrie Andrew Irving. Would they have known that this Australian-born American child would grow to become one of the NBA's most successful players? Perhaps not, but it did not stop Drederick from making basketball an integral part of Kyrie's life.

The Irving family eventually left Melbourne and returned to the United States. The two-year-old Kyrie cannot recall Australia, though his connection to the country has remained a part of his life. Tragedy struck the Irving family when Elizabeth passed away, and Drederick was left to look after Asia and Kyrie by himself.

The basketball court was where the Irving father and son bonded. It was part of Kyrie's life from an early age, but it was in his junior year of high school when he decided he wanted it to become the central focus of his life. However, this love for the sport was on and off. As was the relationship between father and son. Kyrie showed an interest in basketball, but perhaps the constant environment of the sport frustrated him at times. Drederick saw potential in his young son and wanted him to take the sport seriously.

While life at Montclair Kimberly Academy was comfortable, Kyrie was considering changing schools to find a better basketball program. Drederick was pressuring him to decide quickly. The teenager may not have realized and was certainly irritated by his father's insistence to decide immediately. However, as many children eventually realize - their parents knew better! While his skills, guidance by coaches and teammates have contributed to Kyrie's success as a professional basketball player – all credit eventually is owed to Drederick Irving. It was the Boston Terrier who raised the Boston Celtic.

At Home With The Irving's

For someone who has shifted through several homes across cities and even across continents, Kyrie Irving feels there is an emotional connection to a home. However, he states that he is from New Jersey. The Garden State will always be his home. On the program My Houzz he decides to gift his father with a home renovation, using the services provided by the app Houzz. In the program he speaks to the audience about his father's influence. It is here where one can truly understand the influence that Drederick has had on Kyrie.

There are public records which showcase Drederick Irving's achievements as a basketball player. But records do not exist which showcase the sacrifices which parents make for their children. While basketball was not put aside from Drederick's life, it was no longer his priority for himself. As a single father, he wanted to provide daughter Asia and son Kyrie with the best quality of life available.

By a mere half-an-inch, Kyrie is shorter than his father. This forever gives him a height (literally and figuratively) which he still has to reach. While the world may extol the NBA Champion and Olympic Gold medalist, in the smaller, more intimate world of the Irving family, there is another hero, the patriarch Drederick Irving. After retiring from being a professional athlete, Drederick hung up his jersey and exchanged it for a suit and tie. He would work on Wall Street to provide for his family.

Drederick's life was not without its hardships. His father had abandoned him and his five siblings when he was still an infant. Just as he is a single parent, so was his mother, who on welfare managed two jobs to provide for all her children. This made an impression on Drederick and made him into the man he is today. He once remarked to his own son, "I consider myself a good man…but I want you to be a better one."

When Drederick joined Wall Street, he could not imagine that he would survive another great tragedy. He worked as a Financial Broker for Cantor Fitzgerald, which at the time was located in New York City's World Trade Center. He eventually switched to working for Garvan Securities, also in the World Trade Center. However, he was unhappy with this job and shortly left. He finally settled for a position with Thomson Reuters. Though this was at another building, Drederick would walk through the World Trade Center to reach his new office. One morning, he entered the World Trade Center, when the building started to rumble. Debris began to fall from the sky, and the building was being shattered. While he could not make sense of what was happening, he nonetheless dashed out of building with one thought in his mind - he must see his children.

Asia and Kyrie were sitting in school, in a haze of emotions. Parents were flocking into the school picking up their children and taking them home early. Drederick never came. The Irving children remained in school until dismissal and were met by their babysitter when they returned home. The news on television was harrowing. An airplane had flown into the World

Trade Center, destroying it rapidly. Many were killed, and many fled for their lives. Asia and Kyrie were awaiting the news of Drederick's fate. It took Drederick several hours to reach a friend in the Bronx, who called the Irving home and informed the children that their father was safe and on his way home.

Like all Americans, the events of September 11 are etched in Drederick's memory. It is a tragedy from which he managed to escape. Though the children were young, they must have realized the importance of family and what their father meant to them on that very day.

As a young man in the NBA, the lifestyle could get wild. However, Kyrie has a relationship with his father that two friends would have. Even with the extravagant and exciting lifestyle he leads, Kyrie maintains a humility and a simplicity that is rare to find in a young man – especially one who has been showered with the abundance that his professional career has provided him.

This humility and understanding for the more important things in life can be credited to the upbringing by Drederick.

After a renovation by the Houzz team, Kyrie and Asia invite Drederick back into his house to see the changes that were made. They walk him through the living room – now looking more spacious and welcoming. They see the dining room, where the family spends much time together. The wall is adorned with a sign stating: FAMILY FOREVER NO MATTER WHAT

However, the highlight of the renovated house is a room which Asia helped design, unbeknownst to Kyrie. The Irving family walks into a small room in one corner of the large house. The room is adorned with Kyrie's memorabilia from his professional career. Yet these memorabilia are outshined by trophies he received as an amateur, aspiring Basketball player. These are the very trophies which Kyrie left for the garbage collectors to confiscate and destroy forever.

Perhaps now, he is more grateful than ever that they did not collect the cardboard box.

An emotional, teary-eyed Kyrie weeps as he looks around the room. Though the room is dedicated to him, with the name 'Kyrie' adorned on jerseys, trophies, and on a bobble head with his likeness, he can only think of his father, without whom, this room would not exist.

In the now famous First Take interview where Kyrie Irving was grilled about his decision to be traded to the Boston Celtics, he was asked whom should we look to first? Kobe or LeBron? This was referring to who Kyrie's favorite player was.

Without hesitation he stated: "My dad first..."

Perhaps no one could predict that the child born in Kew would become one of basketball's most treasured players. But for the Irving family, the response to who is Kyrie Irving's favorite Basketball player, was obvious.

Chapter Summary

• Drederick Irving left a professional career in Basketball to raise his children.

• The family overcame personal tragedy such as the death of Elizabeth Irving and a scare on the day of the attacks on the World Trade Center.

• As a gift to their father, Kyrie and sister Asia help remodel his house. To Kyrie's surprise, Asia created a room filled with his trophies.

Conclusion

St. Patrick High School closed in 2012. There was a lack of increased enrollment and sadly it caused the school to shut its doors. However, concerned administrators and parents alike wanted to keep the school's legacy alive. They opened a new school and named it The Patrick School. This was non-denominational, yet it would continue to carry the traditions of St. Patrick. And perhaps the greatest tradition is the excellence of the Fighting Celtics, the school's Basketball team. To ensure the students received a first-class training, the gym needed development.

Kyrie Irving may be a Boston Celtic now, but he was a Fighting Celtic as a young teenager. The new slogan of the team is "Once a Celtic, always a Celtic..." and Kyrie Irving seems to have taken this to heart. He funded the renovation of the school's gym and regularly visits the school to spend time with the students and the staff. He is naturally a welcome face on the school grounds as he is remembered as one of St. Patrick's most prestigious alumni; one who has brought immense pride to the school and in particular, to the Fighting Celtics.

Though he does not have a single memory of his birth in Australia, he maintains an affinity for the country. He regularly visits and trains aspiring basketball players in summer programs. While he is no longer with the Cleveland Cavaliers, he remembers the duration of his career with them fondly.

And while the Cleveland Cavaliers may now be his opponents, fans of the team do not shun or forget his contribution to the team and how he helped bring them victory at the NBA Championship. They acknowledge that his contribution was a necessary facet to the team. While LeBron James can no longer offer his former teammate advice due to them being on opposite teams, he wishes Kyrie well, and must continue to acknowledge the skill that his younger counterpart possesses.

The media will always be full of skepticism – it is their responsibility to show different sides of the spectrum. On First Take he was grilled by Stephen A. Smith, but the journalist clearly possess admiration for Kyrie. "He literally looks like a clone...of Kobe Bryant," Smith remarked. After stating on the show that his father was his favorite basketball player, Kyrie stated that his second favorite player was none other than Kobe Bryant.

At first glance, we may feel that we have seen a lot of Kyrie Irving. Yet, he is still in his twenties and has been playing basketball professionally for less than a decade. The discerning viewer will note that we have only seen the beginning – that the NBA Championship, the Olympic Gold Medals, and the current successes with the Boston Celtics are just scratching the surface. The four Uncle Drew short films have led to a feature film, which may become one of many. While Box Office predictions are a complex subject, the buzz around Kyrie Irving and the warm reception toward the short films make one feel optimistic about the future of the feature film.

With the Boston Celtics he has had many successes already. So far, there have also been a few disappointments, of which the major ones were the loss to the Cleveland Cavaliers and the Golden State Warriors. Yet, one must remember that this is only the beginning of Kyrie's career with the Celtics, and that his time with the Cavaliers was not an immediate success. Fans are eager to see him lead the Boston Celtics to the NBA Championship. Just as Drederick Irving brought pride to the city of Boston with his basketball career, all eyes are on Kyrie Irving, and the city is hopeful he will follow in his father's footsteps.

Despite the immense success and fame that he has achieved, Kyrie does not seem to forget his roots. He always credits his father as being the reason for his success.

Kyrie Irving's journey is fascinating: from a small suburb in Australia, to growing up in New Jersey, leading the Cleveland Cavaliers to the Championship. Acquiring Gold Medals at the Olympics and playing for his father's home team in Boston.

Who knows what the future holds for Kyrie Irving, but if his past attainments are an indicator – then his future looks very bright!

Made in the USA
Middletown, DE
15 December 2018